Baby Hats to Crochet

10 FUN DESIGNS FOR NEWBORN TO 12 MONTHS

Kristi Simpson

STACKPOLE BOOKS
Guilford, Connecticut

Published by Stackpole Books
An imprint of The Rowman & Littlefield Publishing Group, Inc.
4501 Forbes Blvd., Ste. 200
Lanham, MD 20706
www.stackpolebooks.com

Distributed by NATIONAL BOOK NETWORK
800-462-6420

Photography of finished items by Lindsay Kubica Photography
Step-by-step photography by Kristi Simpson

We have made every effort to ensure the accuracy and completeness of these instructions. We cannot, however, be responsible for human error, typographical mistakes, or variations in individual work.

This book is a condensed version of *Sweet & Simple Baby Crochet* by Kristi Simpson (2013), which was cataloged by the Library of Congress as follows:

Simpson, Kristi
    Sweet & simple baby crochet / Kristi Simpson. — First edition
        pages cm
    ISBN-13: 978-0-8117-1258-3 (pbk.)
    ISBN-10: 0-8117-1258-3 (pbk.)
    1. Crocheting—Patterns. 2. Infants' clothing. I. Title. II. Title: Sweet and simple baby crochet.
TT820.S5275   2013
746.43'4—dc23

                                                        2013014797

ISBN 978-0-8117-3947-4 (paper : alk. paper)
ISBN 978-0-8117-6941-9 (electronic)

♾™ The paper used in this publication meets the minimum requirements of American National Standard for Information Sciences—Permanence of Paper for Printed Library Materials, ANSI/NISO Z39.48-1992.

First Edition

Contents

How to Read the Patterns

Skill Level

To help you pick a pattern that is consistent with your crochet experience, every pattern in the book indicates its skill level: beginner, moderate beginner, or intermediate. For patterns designated for beginners, you'll need to know how to chain, single crochet, half double crochet, and/or double crochet. As you move up the skill level ladder, more stitch knowledge is required, but it is easy to find help on the internet for any unfamiliar stitches. And none of the patterns is difficult. My design goal is always to create the sweetest items using the simplest stitches possible.

If you are a novice crocheter, let me recommend that you start with Cream Puff Hat (page 14), Football Cocoon and Hat Set (page 22), or Cotton Candy Hat (page 30). These patterns will allow you to practice and perfect the basics before moving onto other stitches and techniques.

Yarn

Under Yarn, you will find listed the specific yarn(s) and colors I used to crochet the pattern, plus how many skeins you'll need. Also included is that specific yarn's "weight." You'll find this information on the label of every skein of yarn you buy, and it ranges from #0 lace weight

Standard Yarn Weight System

Categories of yarn, gauge ranges, and recommended needle and hook sizes

Yarn Weight Symbol & Category Names	0 LACE	1 SUPER FINE	2 FINE	3 LIGHT	4 MEDIUM	5 BULKY	6 SUPER BULKY
Type of Yarns in Category	Fingering 10-Count Crochet Thread	Sock, Fingering, Baby	Sport, Baby	DK, Light Worsted	Worsted, Afghan, Aran	Chunky, Craft, Rug	Bulky, Roving
Knit Gauge Range* in Stockinette Stitch to 4 inches	33–40** sts	27–32 sts	23–26 sts	21–24 sts	16–20 sts	12–15 sts	6–11 sts
Recommended Needle in Metric Size Range	1.5–2.25 mm	2.25–3.25 mm	3.25–3.75 mm	3.75–4.5 mm	4.5–5.5 mm	5.5–8 mm	8 mm and larger
Recommended Needle U.S. Size Range	000–1	1 to 3	3 to 5	5 to 7	7 to 9	9 to 11	11 and larger
Crochet Gauge* Ranges in Single Crochet to 4 inch	32–42 double crochets**	21–32 sts	16–20 sts	12–17 sts	11–14 sts	8–11 sts	5–9 sts
Recommended Hook in Metric Size Range	Steel*** 1.6–1.4 mm	2.25–3.5 mm	3.5–4.5 mm	4.5–5.5 mm	5.5–6.5 mm	6.5–9 mm	9 mm and larger
Recommended Hook U.S. Size Range	Steel*** 6, 7, 8 Regular hook B–1	B–1 to E–4	E–4 to 7	7 to I–9	I–9 to K–10 1/2	K–10 1/2 to M–13	M–13 and larger

*GUIDELINES ONLY: The above reflect the most commonly used gauges and needle or hook sizes for specific yarn categories.

**Lace weight yarns are usually knitted or crocheted on larger needles and hooks to create lacy, openwork patterns. Accordingly, a gauge range is difficult to determine. Always follow the gauge stated in your pattern.

***Steel crochet hooks are sized differently from regular hooks—the higher the number, the smaller the hook, which is the reverse of regular hook sizing.

Source: Craft Yarn Council of America's www.YarnStandards.com

to #6 super bulky weight. If you can't find the specific yarn I used or you'd like to use something else, knowing the yarn weight will let you pick another yarn that will have the same gauge.

Hooks and Other Materials

Here you'll find the hook sizes you'll need, plus any additional materials or tools, which most commonly will include stitch markers, a yarn needle, and a sewing needle and thread.

Gauge

The key to crocheting a garment that fits is to check gauge. Every pattern in this book tells you that project's gauge—namely, how many stitches and rows per inch the final measurements (and final fit) were based on.

To check gauge, you need to crochet a sample swatch using the yarn, hook size, and crochet stitch called for. Crochet the swatch at least 1" larger than required so that you can check the stitches and rows within the swatch to ensure proper gauge. For instance, if the gauge is determined to be 3" square in single crochet, you will work up a swatch in single crochet at least 4" square. Lay a measuring tape on the swatch and count across how many stitches you have in 3". Now reposition the tape and measure up and down how many rows you have in 3".

If you have more stitches and rows than you should, try the next larger hook size, and make another gauge swatch. Keep doing this until the swatch matches the pattern gauge. If you have fewer stitches and rows than you should, retest your gauge with the next size smaller hook in same way.

Notes

Be sure to read the Notes section before beginning a project. You'll find helpful hints there, including what stitches beyond the basic single crochet and double crochet might be used.

Special Techniques

A few of the patterns include stitch tutorials, which you'll find under Special Techniques. In most cases, these stitches are particular to that specific pattern.

Directions

- When a number is before the command, such as 3hdc, you will work in the SAME stitch.
- When a number is after the command, such as hdc3, you will work that command in that number of following stitches.
- The number in parentheses at the end of a round or row is the TOTAL number of stitches for that round or row.
- An asterisk will mark a specific starting point for repeating a section in a pattern.
- Working "in the round" means that you will be working in one direction throughout, not back and forth in rows. Working "continuously in the round" means that the rounds will be crocheted without joining.
- When you see commands written within a set of parentheses, all those commands will be crocheted in the same stitch—for example, "(ch1, dc, ch1) in the next stitch."

Abbreviations

ch	chain
dc	double crochet
dc dec	double crochet decrease
dec	decrease
flo	front loop only
hdc	half double crochet
inc	increase
sc	single crochet
sc dec	single crochet decrease
sl st	slip stitch
st(s)	stitch(es)
tr	treble crochet

Emily Cluster Hat

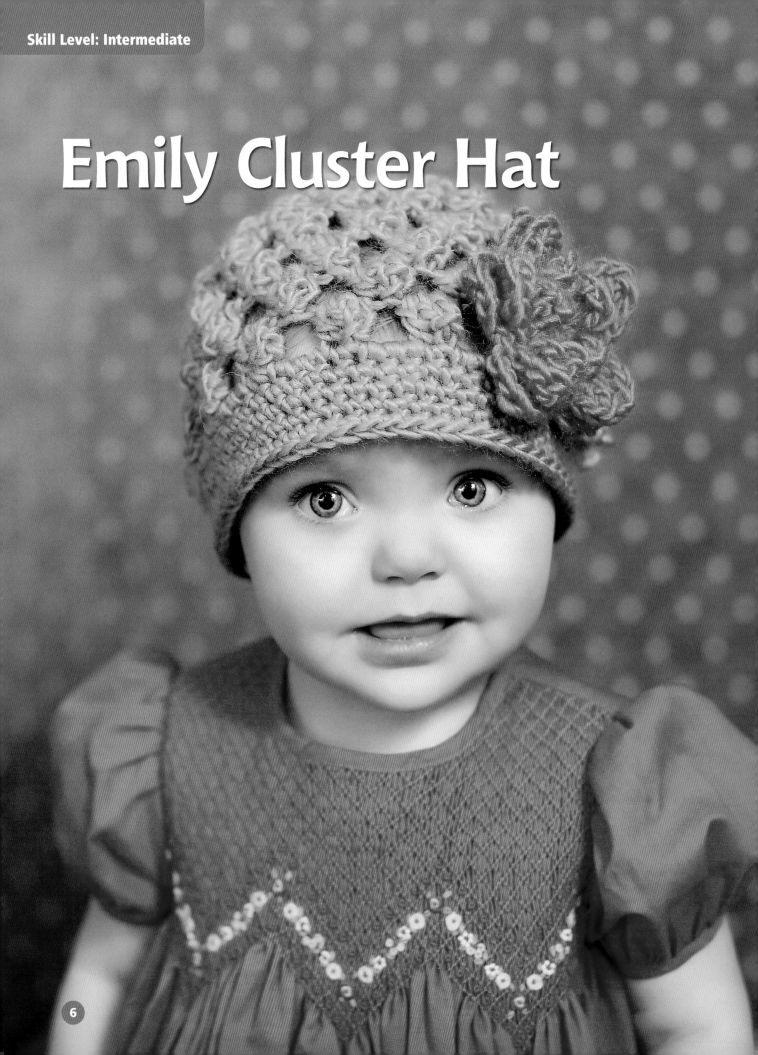

Every little girl needs a hat that can be worn in each season, and this is it.
Make it in a variety of colors to complete your little girl's accessory wardrobe.

Finished Measurements
6–12 months: Circumference, 18"; Hat height, 6"
(For other sizes, see Notes.)

Yarn
- Caron Sheep(ish) by Vickie Howell, medium worsted
  weight #4 yarn, 70% acrylic/30% wool (167 yd/3 oz
  per skein)
    1 skein #7 Turquoise(ish) (Color A)
    1 skein #17 Pink(ish) (Color B)

Hook and Other Materials
- K-10½ 6.5mm hook or size needed to obtain gauge
- Yarn needle

Gauge
11 sts and 14 rows in sc = 4" square

Notes
1. The hat is worked from the top down in the round.
2. The first ch3 of each round counts as a dc throughout
   the pattern.
3. The size can be made smaller or larger by using a
   smaller or larger hook to decrease or increase gauge.

Special Technique
Cluster
4dc, sl st to first dc. The sl st will join the 4 stitches into
1 stitch, creating a cluster.

Hat

Using Color A, ch4, sl st to first chain to create a ring.
Round 1: Ch3 (counts as first dc here and throughout),
    3dc in ring, sl st to third chain of ch3 to make first clus-
    ter, ch3, cluster (see Special Technique), ch3, cluster,
    ch3, cluster, ch3, sl st to third chain of first ch3 to join
    round (16 sts).
Round 2: Ch3, 3dc in last ch3 space of previous round, sl
    st to third chain of first ch3 to make first cluster, *ch3,
    (cluster, ch3, cluster) in next ch3 space from previous
    round, repeat from * to last ch3 space. To finish, ch3, sl
    st to third chain of first ch3 (8 clusters and 8 ch3 spaces
    created for a total of 32 sts).
Round 3: Ch3, 3dc in last ch3 space of previous round, sl
    st to third chain of first ch3 to make first cluster, *ch3,
    (cluster, ch3, cluster) in next ch3 space from previous
    round, repeat from * to last ch3 space. To finish, ch3,
    sl st to third chain of first ch3 (16 clusters and 16 ch3
    spaces created for a total of 64 sts).
Round 4: Ch3, 3dc in last ch3 space of previous round, sl
    st to third chain of first ch3 to make first cluster, *ch1,

cluster in ch3 space of previous round, ch1, cluster in
ch3 space of previous round, repeat from * to complete
round, ch1, sl st to third chain of first ch3 to join (32 sts).
Round 5: Ch3, 3dc in last ch1 space of previous round, sl
st to third chain of first ch3 to make first cluster, *ch1,
cluster in ch1 space of previous round, ch1, cluster in
ch1 space of previous round, repeat from * to complete
round, ch1, sl st to third chain of first ch3 to join (32 sts).
Rounds 6–8: Repeat Round 5.
Round 9: Ch1, sc in each stitch (32 sts).
Rounds 10–13: Working continuously in the round, repeat
    Round 9. To finish, sl st to first stitch of round.
Fasten off. Weave in ends.

Flowers
Top Flower
Using Color B, ch4, sl st to first chain to create a ring.
Round 1: Ch1, 5sc in ring, do not join (5 sts).
Round 2: Sl st to first stitch. In same stitch (ch1, hdc, dc,
    tr, dc, hdc, ch1, sl st), *sl st to next stitch and in same
    stitch (ch1, hdc, dc, tr, dc, hdc, ch1, sl st), repeat from *
    to complete 5 petals.
To finish, sl st to first ch1 to complete first level.
Do not fasten off; work straight into Middle Flower.

Middle Flower
Round 1: Ch1, 5sc in ring, do not join (5 sts).
Round 2: Sl st to first stitch. In same stitch (ch1, hdc, dc,
    tr, dc, hdc, ch1, sl st), *sl st to next stitch and in same
    stitch (ch1, hdc, dc, tr, dc, hdc, ch1, sl st), repeat from *
    to complete 5 petals.
Round 3: *Ch3, sl st to slip stitch created in between the
    petals, repeat from * around the flower. It can be in
    front of the petals, because it will form correctly and lie
    flat when finished. After completing the 5 ch3 sections,
    work right into the petals.
Round 4: Sl st to first ch3 space, work (ch1, hdc, dc, tr, dc,
    hdc, ch1, sl st) in space, *sl st to next ch3 space, work
    (ch1, hdc, dc, tr, dc, hdc, ch1, sl st) in space, repeat
    from * to complete 5 petals.
To finish, sl st to first ch1.
Do not fasten off; work straight into Back Flower.

Back Flower
Repeat Middle Flower.
Fasten off. Weave in ends.
Arrange flower levels on top of one another so that the
    petals all lie correctly and are not hidden behind the
    others. Attach the flower with yarn needle to hat.

Puppy Hat

"How cute is that puppy!" Yes, that's exactly what your friends
and family will be saying every time they see your baby in this hat.

Finished Measurements

Newborn: Circumference, 12–14"; Hat height, 5.5–6"

3–6 months: Circumference, 14–17"; Hat height, 6.5–7"

9–12 months: Circumference, 16–19"; Hat height, 7.5"

Yarn

- Lion Brand Jiffy, bulky weight #5 yarn, 100% acrylic
  (135 yd/3 oz per skein)
    - 1 skein #450-126 Espresso (Color A)
    - 1 skein #450-098 Oat (Color B)

Hook and Other Materials

- H-8 5mm hook or size needed to obtain gauge
- Yarn needle
- 2 small black buttons (for the eyes)
- 1 large black button (for the nose)
- Sewing thread and needle

Gauge

9 sts and 12 rows in hdc = 3" square

Notes

1. You will make the hat and all the parts first. The ears, eyes, and spots will be added last using a yarn needle.
2. The hat is worked from the top down continuously in the round. If you like, mark the first stitch of the round with a stitch marker for reference.
3. The ears can be made longer or shorter by increasing or decreasing the length of Rows 8–33.

Hat

Newborn

Using Color A, ch4, sl st to first chain to create a ring.

Round 1: Ch2 (this counts as your first hdc), 7hdc in ring (8 sts).

Round 2: Working continuously in the round, 2hdc in each stitch (16 sts).

Round 3: *Hdc, 2hdc in next stitch, repeat from * to complete round (24 sts).

Round 4: *Hdc2, 2hdc in next stitch, repeat from * to complete round (32 sts).

Rounds 5–16: Hdc in each stitch, sl st to first stitch of round to join (32 sts).

Fasten off. Weave in ends.

3–6 Months

Using Color A, ch4, sl st to first chain to create a ring.

Round 1: Ch2 (this counts as your first hdc), 7hdc in ring (8 sts).

Round 2: Working continuously in the round, 2hdc in each stitch (16 sts).

Round 3: *Hdc, 2hdc in next stitch, repeat from * to complete round (24 sts).

Round 4: *Hdc2, 2hdc in next stitch, repeat from * to complete round (32 sts).

Round 5: *Hdc3, 2hdc in next stitch, repeat from * to complete round (40 sts).

Rounds 6–20: Hdc in each stitch, sl st to first stitch of round to join (40 sts).

Fasten off. Weave in ends.

9–12 Months

Using Color A, ch4, sl st to first chain to create a ring.

Round 1: Ch2 (this counts as your first hdc), 7hdc in ring (8 sts).

Round 2: Working continuously in the round, 2hdc in each stitch (16 sts).

Round 3: *Hdc, 2hdc in next stitch, repeat from * to complete round (24 sts).

Round 4: *Hdc2, 2hdc in next stitch, repeat from * to complete round (32 sts).

Round 5: *Hdc3, 2hdc in next stitch, repeat from * to complete round (40 sts).

Round 6: *Hdc4, 2hdc in next stitch, repeat from * to complete round (48 sts).

Rounds 7–24: Hdc in each stitch, sl st to first stitch of round to join (48 sts).

Fasten off. Weave in ends.

Eye Patch

Using Color B, ch4, sl st to first chain to create a ring.

Round 1: Ch1, 5sc in ring (6 sts).

Round 2: Working continuously in the round, 2sc in each stitch (12 sts).

Round 3: *Sc, 2sc in next stitch, repeat from * to complete round (18 sts).

Round 4: *Sc2, 2sc in next stitch, repeat from * to complete round (24 sts). Sl st to first stitch of round to join.

Fasten off, leaving a long tail to sew onto hat. Weave in other end.

Ear Spot

Using Color B, ch4, sl st to first chain to create a ring.

Round 1: Ch1, 5sc in ring (6 sts).

Round 2: 2sc in each stitch (12 sts). Sl st to first stitch of round to join.

Fasten off, leaving a long tail to sew onto ear. Weave in other end.

Ears (make 1 in each color)

Ch5.

Row 1: Turn, sc in first chain and across (4 sts).

Row 2: Turn, ch1, sc in first stitch and across (4 sts).

Rows 3–6: Repeat Row 2.

Row 7: Turn, ch1, sc in same stitch, sc across to next to last stitch, 2sc in last stitch (6 sts).

Rows 8–33: Turn, ch1, sc in first stitch and across (6 sts).

Row 34: Turn, sc dec, sc2, sc dec (4 sts).

Fasten off. Weave in ends.

Ear Trim

With the front side of the ear facing you, join Color A at top left at first chain. Using ends of rows as stitches, ch1, sc around ear, sl st to ch1 to join.

Fasten off, leaving a long tail to sew onto hat. Weave in other end.

Repeat with the other ear.

Finishing

Sew each ear onto the hat 3 rows down from the top of the beanie. Sew the eye patch onto 1 side. Sew the ear spot onto 1 of the ears. To finish, using sewing needle and thread, sew the 2 small buttons on for eyes and the 1 large button on for the nose. Weave in ends.

Aviator Cap

We all love to see our little ones soar, and now they can do it wearing this sweet aviator cap!

Finished Measurements

Newborn: Circumference, 12–14";
    Hat height, 5.5–6"

3–6 months: Circumference, 14–17";
    Hat height, 6.5–7"

9–12 months: Circumference, 16–19";
    Hat height, 7.5"

Yarn

- Lion Brand Jiffy, bulky weight #5 yarn, 100% acrylic (135 yd/3 oz per skein)

      1 skein #450-126 Espresso
      (Color A)

      1 skein #450-098 Oat (Color B)

Hook and Other Materials

- H-8 5mm or size need to obtain gauge
- Yarn needle
- Stitch markers

Gauge

9 sts and 12 rows in sc = 3" square

Notes

1. The hat is worked from the top down continuously in the round. If you like, use a stitch marker to mark the first stitch of the round for reference.
2. The goggles are made separately and sewn onto the hat with a yarn needle.
3. The headband is attached to the goggles, not to the hat, so it will stretch when worn.

Hat

Newborn

Using Color A, ch4, sl st to first chain to create a ring.

Round 1: Ch1 (this counts as your first sc), 7sc in ring (8 sts).

Round 2: Working continuously in the round, 2sc in each stitch (16 sts).

Round 3: *Sc, 2sc in next stitch, repeat from * to complete round (24 sts).

Round 4: *Sc2, 2sc in next stitch, repeat from * to complete round (32 sts).

Rounds 5–16: Sc in each stitch (32 sts).

Fasten off and weave in ends.

3–6 Months

Using Color A, ch4, sl st to first chain to create a ring.

Round 1: Ch1 (this counts as your first sc), 7sc in ring (8 sts).

Round 2: Working continuously in the round, 2sc in each stitch (16 sts).

Round 3: *Sc, 2sc in next stitch, repeat from * to complete round (24 sts).

Round 4: *Sc2, 2sc in next stitch, repeat from * to complete round (32 sts).

Round 5: *Sc3, 2sc in next stitch, repeat from * to complete round (40 sts).

Rounds 6–20: Sc in each stitch (40 sts).

Fasten off and weave in ends.

9–12 Months

Using Color A, ch4, sl st to first chain to create a ring.

Round 1: Ch1 (this counts as your first sc), 7sc in ring (8 sts).

Round 2: Working continuously in the round, 2sc in each stitch (16 sts).

Round 3: *Sc, 2sc in next stitch, repeat from * to complete round (24 sts).

Round 4: *Sc2, 2sc in next stitch, repeat from * to complete round (32 sts).

Round 5: *Sc3, 2sc in next stitch, repeat from * to complete round (40 sts).

Round 6: *Sc4, 2sc in next stitch, repeat from * to complete round (48 sts).

Rounds 7–24: Sc in each stitch (48 sts).

Fasten off and weave in ends.

Ear Flaps (make 2)

Fold hat in half and mark opposite sides on the last round with a stitch marker. Join Color A at marker and follow pattern per size to complete ear flaps.

Newborn

Using Color A, ch1.

Row 1: 6sc (6 sts).

Rows 2–5: Turn, ch1, sc to end of row (6 sts).

Row 6: Turn, sc dec, sc2, sc dec (4 sts).

Row 7: Turn, sc dec, sc dec (2 sts).

Fasten off. Weave in ends.

Repeat for flap on opposite side.

3–6 and 9–12 Months

Using Color A, ch1.

Row 1: 8sc (8 sts).

Rows 2–6: Turn, ch1, sc to end of row (8 sts).

Row 7: Turn, sc dec, sc4, sc dec (6 sts).

Row 8: Turn, sc dec, sc2, sc dec (4 sts).

Fasten off. Weave in ends.

Repeat for flap on opposite side.

Goggles (all sizes; make 2)

Using Color B, ch20, sl st to first chain to make a ring.

Round 1: Ch1, sc in each chain, sl st to ch1 to join.

Fasten off. Weave in ends.

With yarn needle, sew rings onto the hat in 2 oval shapes, touching at one end to create the goggles. For the nose piece, use Color B and wrap around where the ovals touch 10 times. This will also make the goggles look seamless.

Fasten off. Weave in ends.

Headband

Lay the hat in front of you. Join Color B on outside middle of the right goggle, ch35 (ch40 for 3–6 months/ch45 for 9–12 months), sl st to the middle of the left goggle. Turn the hat and sl st to the stitch below on the goggles. Now sc in each chain back across the headband. Sl st to the stitch below the first chain made on the right side of goggle. Fasten off. Weave in ends.

Cream Puff Hat

I love to mix yarns to create wonderful textures. Using basic stitches,
you can crochet a stunning accessory that will amaze you and your friends.

Finished Measurements
Newborn: Circumference, 12–14"; Hat height, 5.5–6"
3–6 months: Circumference, 14–17"; Hat height, 6.5–7"
9–12 months: Circumference, 16–19"; Hat height, 7.5"

Yarn
• Bernat Giggles, medium worsted weight #4 yarn,
  90% acrylic/10% nylon (185 yd/3.5 oz per skein)
      1 skein #56510 Cheery Cream (Color A)
• Heartstrings by Dee Thick and Thin
  (*HeartstringsbyDee.etsy.com*), super bulky #6 yarn,
  100% merino (15 yd/1.5 oz per skein)
      1 skein Rusty Peach Colorway (Color B)

Hook and Other Materials
• H-8 5mm hook or size needed to obtain gauge
• Stitch marker (optional)
• Yarn needle

Gauge
Using Color A, 14 sts and 16 rows in sc = 4" square

Notes
1. The hat is worked from the bottom up continuously
   in the round. If you like, mark the first stitch of each
   round with a stitch marker for reference.
2. When using the Thick and Thin yarn, work loosely so
   that the texture stays intact. If the yarn is pulled tight,
   the texture will not be seen.
3. When you change from Color A to Color B, you will
   carry Color A, not fasten it off. That will allow you to
   simply pick the yarn up later, with no ends to weave in.
   (Because of its thickness, Color B is too difficult to carry,
   so it gets fastened off each time.)

Hat
Newborn
Using Color A, ch39.
Round 1: Sc in first chain and in each ch around, sl st to
    first chain to create a ring (38 sts).
Round 2: Ch1, sc in each stitch around; do not join (38 sts).
Rounds 3–6: Working continuously in the round, sc in
    each stitch (38 sts).
Drop Color A (see Notes); join Color B.
Round 7: *Sc, dc, repeat from * to complete round (38 sts).
Fasten off Color B; pick up Color A.
Rounds 8–9: Sc in each stitch (38 sts).
Round 10: Repeat Round 7.
Drop Color A; join Color B.

Rounds 11–17: Sc in each stitch (38 sts). To finish, sl st to
    first stitch of round.
Fasten off, leaving a long tail to sew top together.
Using yarn needle, sew the top together.

3–6 Months
Using Color A, ch45.
Round 1: Sc in first chain and in each ch around, sl st to
    first chain to create a ring (44 sts).
Round 2: Ch1, sc in each stitch to complete round, do not
    join (44 sts).
Rounds 3–6: Working continuously in the round, sc in
    each stitch (44 sts).
Drop Color A (see Notes); join Color B.
Round 7: *Sc, dc, repeat from * to complete round (44 sts).
Fasten off Color B; pick up Color A.
Rounds 8–9: Sc in each stitch (44 sts).
Round 10: Repeat Round 7.
Drop Color A; join Color B.
Rounds 11–20: Sc in each stitch (44 sts). To finish, sl st to
    first stitch of round.
Fasten off, leaving a long tail to sew top together.
Using yarn needle, sew the top together.

9–12 Months
Using Color A, ch51.
Round 1: Sc in first chain and in each ch around, sl st to
    first chain to create a ring (50 sts).
Round 2: Ch1, sc in each stitch to complete round; do not
    join (50 sts).
Rounds 3–8: Working continuously in the round, sc in
    each stitch (50 sts).
Drop Color A; join Color B.
Round 9: *Sc, dc, repeat from * to complete round (50 sts).
Fasten off Color B; pick up Color A.
Rounds 10–11: Sc in each stitch (50 sts).
Round 12: Repeat Round 9.
Drop Color A; join Color B.
Rounds 13–25: Sc in each stitch (50 sts). To finish, sl st to
    first stitch of round.
Fasten off, leaving a long tail to sew top together.
Using yarn needle, sew top together.

Tassels (make 2)
Make 2 tassels using Color A. Tie the tassels to the corners
of the hat.

Knotty Flower Twist

This sweet hat is a fun twist on the traditional beanie. The little knot topped off with a flower will surely bring a smile to any new mom!

Finished Measurements
Newborn: Circumference, 12–14"; Hat height, 5.5–6"

Yarn
• Peaches & Creme, medium worsted weight #4 yarn, 100% cotton (120 yd/2.5 oz per skein)
    1 skein #1740 Bright Pink (Color A)
    1 skein #1712 Bright Lime (Color B)
    1 skein #1612 Sunshine (Color C)

Hook and Other Materials
• H-8 5mm hook or size needed to obtain gauge
• Stitch marker (optional)

Gauge
10 sts and 14 rows in sc = 4" square

Notes
1. You can make the hat in 1 solid color, with various stripes, or as directed.
2. The hat is worked from the top down continuously in the round. If you like, mark the first stitch of the round with a stitch marker for reference.
3. The flower is added at the end.
4. To change colors, push hook through the next stitch, pull yarn back through, yarn over with the NEXT color, and pull through. Color change is complete.

Hat

Using Color A, ch4, sl st to first chain to create a ring.
Round 1: Ch1, sc in each chain (4 sts).
Rounds 2–25: Working continuously in the round, sc in each stitch (4 sts).
Round 26: 2sc in each stitch (8 sts).
Round 27: *Sc, 2sc in next stitch, repeat from * to complete round (12 sts).
Round 28: *Sc, 2sc in next stitch, repeat from * to complete round (18 sts).
Round 29: *Sc2, 2sc in next stitch, repeat from * to complete round (24 sts).
Round 30: *Sc3, 2sc in next stitch, repeat from * to complete round (30 sts).
Round 31: *Sc4, 2sc in next stitch, repeat from * to complete round (36 sts).
Rounds 32–45: Sc in each stitch (36 sts).
Fasten off Color A. Join Color B.
Round 46: Sc in each stitch (36 sts).
Fasten off Color B. Join Color C.

Round 47: Sc in each stitch, sl st to first stitch of round to join (36 sts).
Fasten off. Weave in ends.

Flower

Join Color B at end of tube on top of the hat.
Round 1: Ch1, sc in each chain, sl st to first ch1 to join (6 sts).
Round 2: In first stitch, (ch1, 2dc, ch1) and sl st to same stitch, *sl st to next stitch, (ch1, 2dc, ch1) in stitch, and sl st to same stitch, repeat from * to complete the petals (6 petals). Sl st to first ch1 of first petal to join.
Fasten off. Weave in ends to back of flower.
Using posts of the sc from Round 1, join Color B, loosely sl st around, and sl st to first slip stitch to join.
Fasten off. Weave in ends to back of flower.
Knot the tube loosely to finish.

Elephant Ears Beanie

Not only is this beanie adorable, but it can also be personalized for a boy or girl. You'll be the hit of the baby shower.

Finished Measurements

Newborn: Circumference, 12–14"; Hat height, 5.5–6"
3–6 months: Circumference, 14–17"; Hat height, 6.5–7"
9–12 months: Circumference, 16–19"; Hat height, 7.5"

Yarn

- Red Heart Super Saver, medium worsted weight #4 yarn, 100% acrylic (364 yd/7 oz)
  - 1 skein #3950 Charcoal (Color A)
  - 1 skein #373 Petal Pink (Color B)

Hook and Other Materials

- H-8 5mm hook or size needed to obtain gauge
- Yarn needle
- Stitch markers

Gauge

10 sts and 9 rows in sc = 3" square

Notes

1. The beanie is worked from the top down continuously in the round. If you like, mark the first stitch of the round with a stitch marker for reference.
2. The beanie and ears are made separately and sewn together.

Special Technique

Cluster

1. Yarn over, push hook through stitch, yarn over, and pull yarn back through: 3 loops on hook.

2. Yarn over, pull yarn through first 2 loops: 2 loops on hook.

3. Yarn over, push hook through SAME stitch, yarn over, and pull yarn back through: 4 loops on hook.

4. Yarn over, pull yarn through first 2 loops: 3 loops on hook.

5. Yarn over, pull yarn through all stitches. Cluster is complete.

Beanie

Newborn

Using Color A, ch4, sl st to first chain to create a ring.

Round 1: Ch1 (this counts as your first sc), 7sc in ring (8 sts).

Round 2: Working continuously in the round, 2hdc (see Notes) in each stitch (16 sts).

Round 3: *Sc, 2sc in next stitch, repeat from * to complete round (24 sts).

Round 4: *Hdc2, 2hdc in next stitch, repeat from * to complete round (32 sts).

Round 5: Sc in each stitch (32 sts).

Round 6: Hdc in each stitch (32 sts).

Rounds 7–16: Repeat Rounds 5 and 6. To finish, sl st to first stitch of round.

Fasten off. Weave in ends.

3–6 Months

Using Color A, ch4, sl st to first chain to create a ring.

Round 1: Ch1 (this counts as your first sc), 7sc in ring (8 sts).

Round 2: Working continuously in the round, 2hdc (see Notes) in each stitch (16 sts).

Round 3: *Sc, 2sc in next stitch, repeat from * to complete round (24 sts).

Round 4: *Hdc2, 2hdc in next stitch, repeat from * to complete round (32 sts).

Round 5: *Sc3, 2sc in next stitch, repeat from * to complete round (40 sts).

Round 6: Hdc in each stitch (40 sts).

Round 7: Sc in each stitch (40 sts).

Rounds 8–20: Repeat Rounds 6 and 7. To finish, sl st to first stitch of round.

Fasten off. Weave in ends.

9–12 Months

Using Color A, ch4, sl st to first chain to create a ring.

Round 1: Ch1 (this counts as your first sc), 7sc in ring (8 sts).

Round 2: Working continuously in the round, 2hdc (see Notes) in each stitch (16 sts).

Round 3: *Sc, 2sc in next stitch, repeat from * to complete round (24 sts).

Round 4: *Hdc2, 2hdc in next stitch, repeat from * to complete round (32 sts).

Round 5: *Sc3, 2sc in next stitch, repeat from * to complete round (40 sts).

Round 6: *Hdc4, 2hdc in next stitch, repeat from * to complete round (48 sts).

Round 7: Sc in each stitch (48 sts).

Round 8: Hdc in each stitch (48 sts).

Rounds 9–24: Repeat Rounds 7 and 8. To finish, sl st to first stitch of round.

Fasten off. Weave in ends.

Ears

Make 2 of each section, 1 in each color. To make the ears for 3–6 months, repeat the last round for the top and bottom parts one time. To make the ears for 6–12 months, repeat the last round for the top and bottom parts twice.

Newborn

Top

Ch2.

Round 1: 6sc in first chain (6 sts).

Round 2: Working in the round, 2sc in each stitch (12 sts).

Round 3: *Sc, 2sc in next stitch, repeat from * to complete round (18 sts).

Round 4: *Sc2, 2sc in next stitch, repeat from * to complete round (24 sts).

Fasten off.

Bottom

Ch2.

Round 1: 6sc in first chain (6 sts).

Round 2: Working in the round, 2sc in each stitch (12 sts).

Round 3: *Sc, 2sc in next stitch, repeat from * to complete round (18 sts). Fasten off.

Using 4 stitches to join, sew the top and bottom sections of each color together with the yarn needle.

Next, sew the pink onto the gray, making it 1 piece.

Next, trim will be added to the outside of each ear.

Right Ear

Place 1 ear in front of you, pink side up, with the smaller side closest to you. Locate the center stitch at the bottom and count 4 stitches to the left. Place a stitch marker. Now locate the center stitch at the top of the ear, count 6 stitches to the left, and place a marker.

At the marker on the bottom, join Color A, ch3, and cluster (see Special Technique on page 19) in each stitch around the outside of the ear. When you reach the center point where the circles join, sl st and then cluster in each stitch around the top section until you reach the second stitch marker. Fasten off.

Left Ear

Place the other ear in front of you, pink side up, with the smaller side closest to you. Locate the center stitch at the bottom and count 4 stitches to the right. Place a stitch marker. Now locate the center stitch at the top of the ear, count 6 stitches to the right, and place a marker.

At the marker on the bottom, join Color A, ch3, and cluster (see Special Technique) in each stitch around the outside of the ear. When you reach the center point where the circles join, sl st and then cluster in each stitch around the top section until you reach the second stitch marker. Fasten off.

Sew the ears onto the hat with the yarn needle. Weave in ends.

Hair Sprigs

Cut 8 to 10 lengths of Color A approximately 4" long. Fold the lengths in half, pull the folded center of the lengths through the first ch4 ring, and finish by pulling the ends through the loop (like fringe). Trim evenly.

1. Push hook through first round of hat, and pull center of yarn strands through.

2. Pull ends of strands through loop and pull tight. Repeat around ring.

3. Trim evenly.

Football Cocoon and Hat Set

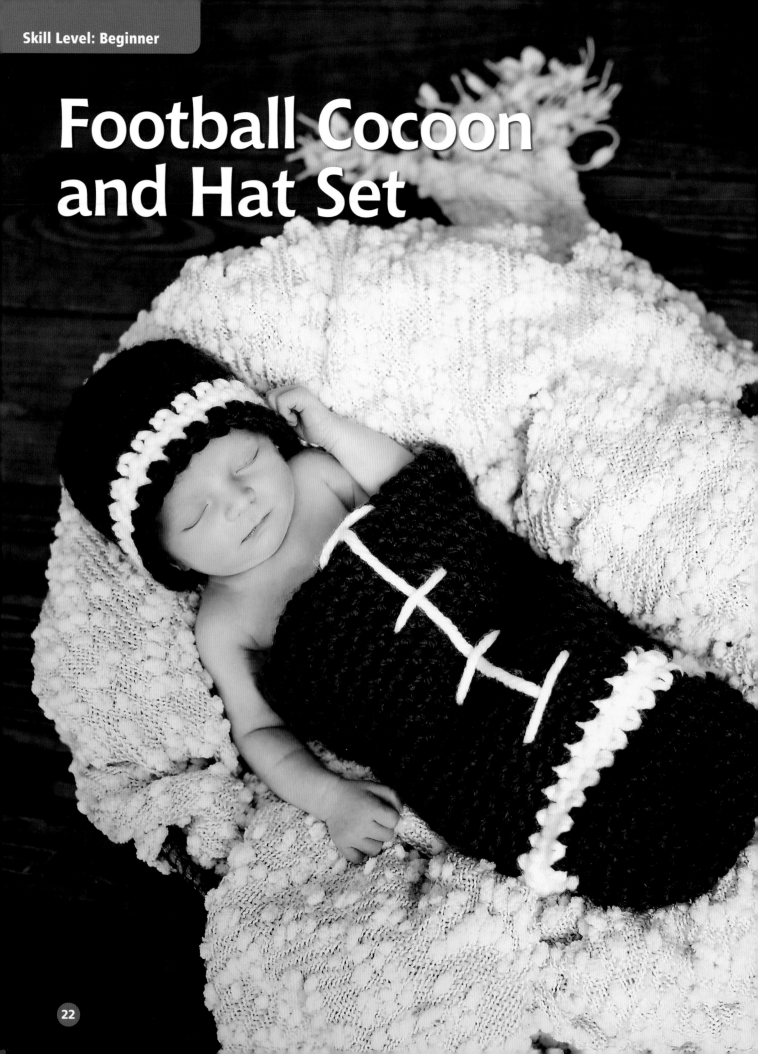

For all the football fans, this set is a must-have. It is the perfect shower gift as well as a fun way to celebrate a game at home. And being from Alabama, I'll be the first to say, "Roll Tide!"

Finished Measurements
Cocoon: Length, 20"; Circumference, 16.5"
Hat: Circumference, 12.5"; Height, 5.5"

Yarn
- Lion Brand Hometown USA, super bulky #6 yarn, 100% acrylic (81 yd/5 oz per skein)
  - 2 skeins #135-125 Billings Chocolate (Color A)
  - 1 skein #135-100 New York White (Color B)

Hook and Other Materials
- N-13 9mm hook or size needed to obtain gauge
- Stitch marker (optional)

Gauge
8 sts and 9 rows in sc = 4" square

Notes
1. Cocoon is worked in the round and is joined by a slip stitch until Round 7, when you work continuously in the round.
2. Ch1 at beginning of each round counts as a stitch.
3. When you change yarns, you will carry the old yarn, not fasten it off. That will allow you to simply drop and pick the yarn up later, with no ends to weave in.
4. The football seams are added after the cocoon is finished.
5. The cocoon length can be increased by increasing the finished rows.
6. Hat is worked from the top down. From Round 4 it is worked continuously in the round. If you like, mark the first stitch of the round with a stitch marker for reference.

Cocoon
Using Color A, ch4, sl st to first chain to make a ring.
Round 1: Ch1 (counts as a stitch here and throughout), 5sc in ring, sl st to ch1 to join (6 sts).
Round 2: Ch1, sc in same stitch, 2sc in each stitch to complete round, sl st to ch1 to join (12 sts).
Round 3: Ch1, 2sc in next stitch, *sc, 2sc in next stitch, repeat from * to complete round, sl st to ch1 to join (18 sts).
Round 4: Ch1, sc, 2sc in next stitch, *sc2, 2sc in next stitch, repeat from * to complete round, sl st to ch1 to join (24 sts).

Round 5: Ch1, sc2, 2sc in next stitch, *sc3, 2sc in next stitch, repeat from * to complete round, sl st to ch1 to join (30 sts).
Round 6: Ch1, sc3, 2sc in next stitch, *sc4, 2sc in next stitch, repeat from * to complete round, sl st to ch1 to join (36 sts).
Rounds 7–10: Working continuously in the round, sc in each stitch (36 sts).
Join Color B; drop Color A (see Notes).
Rounds 11–12: Working continuously in the round, sc in each stitch (36 sts).
Fasten off Color B; pick up Color A.
Rounds 13–30: Working continuously in the round, sc in each stitch (36 sts). To finish, sl st to next stitch.
Fasten off. Weave in ends.

Football Seams
With the crochet hook, pull Color B through the third row above the white stripe and the third row from the top. Slip stitch to secure it into place on the inside at both ends. Cut five 6" lengths of Color B. Thread each piece perpendicular to the piece you've already secured, spacing them evenly and centering them. Slip stitch to secure them on each end on the inside. Trim the ends on the inside, and the football cocoon is complete.

Hat
Using Color A, ch4, sl st to first chain to make a ring.
Round 1: Ch1, 5sc in ring, sl st to ch1 to join (6 sts).
Round 2: Ch1, sc in same stitch, 2sc in each stitch to complete round, sl st to ch1 to join (12 sts).
Round 3: Ch1, 2sc in next stitch, *sc, 2sc in next stitch, repeat from * to complete round, sl st to ch1 to join (18 sts).
Rounds 4–9: Working continuously in the round, sc in each stitch (18 sts).
Join Color B; drop Color A (see Notes).
Rounds 10–11: Working continuously in the round, sc in each stitch (18 sts).
Fasten off Color B; pick up Color A.
Round 12: Working continuously in the round, sc in each stitch (18 sts). To finish, sl st to next stitch.
Fasten off. Weave in ends.

Giraffe Hat

Perfect for boys or girls, this giraffe hat is a must-make!

Finished Measurements

Newborn: Circumference, 12–14";
    Hat height, 5.5–6"

3–6 months: Circumference, 14–17";
    Hat height, 6.5–7"

9–12 months: Circumference, 16–19";
    Hat height, 7.5"

Yarn

- Red Heart Super Saver, medium worsted weight #4 yarn, 100% acrylic (364 yd/7 oz per skein)
  - 1 skein #0320 Cornmeal (Color A)
  - 1 skein #0365 Coffee (Color B)
  - 1 skein #0336 Warm Brown (Color C)

Hook and Other Materials

- H-8 5mm hook or size needed to obtain gauge
- Stitch markers
- Yarn needle
- Two 1" black buttons
- Sewing thread and needle

Gauge

11 sts and 14 rows in sc = 4" square

Notes

1. The hat is worked from the top down continuously in the round. If you like, mark the first stitch of the round with a stitch marker for your reference.
2. The gauge should be loose for this pattern, so please check before beginning.
3. The eyes, ears, and horns will be added to the hat separately. The foundation row of the nose is crocheted right onto the hat and then the rest is sewn on.

Hat

Newborn

Using Color A, ch4, sl st to first chain to create a ring.

Round 1: Ch1 (this counts as your first sc), 7sc in ring (8 sts).

Round 2: Working continuously in the round, 2sc in each stitch (16 sts).

Round 3: *Sc, 2sc in next stitch, repeat from * to complete round (24 sts).

Round 4: *Sc2, 2sc in next stitch, repeat from * to complete round (32 sts).

Rounds 5–16: Sc in each stitch (32 sts). To finish, sl st to first stitch of round.

Fasten off. Weave in ends.

3–6 Months

Using Color A, ch4, sl st to first chain to create a ring.

Round 1: Ch1 (this counts as your first sc), 7sc in ring (8 sts).

Round 2: Working continuously in the round, 2sc in each stitch (16 sts).

Round 3: *Sc, 2sc in next stitch, repeat from * to complete round (24 sts).

Round 4: *Sc2, 2sc in next stitch, repeat from * to complete round (32 sts).

Round 5: *Sc3, 2sc in next stitch, repeat from * to complete round (40 sts).

Rounds 6–20: Sc in each stitch (40 sts). To finish, sl st to first stitch of round.

Fasten off. Weave in ends.

9–12 Months

Using Color A, ch4, sl st to first chain to create a ring.

Round 1: Ch1 (this counts as your first sc), 7sc in ring (8 sts).

Round 2: Working continuously in the round, 2sc in each stitch (16 sts).

Round 3: *Sc, 2sc in next stitch, repeat from * to complete round (24 sts).

Round 4: *Sc2, 2sc in next stitch, repeat from * to complete round (32 sts).

Round 5: *Sc3, 2sc in next stitch, repeat from * to complete round (40 sts).

Round 6: *Sc4, 2sc in next stitch, repeat from * to complete round (48 sts).

Rounds 7–24: Sc in each stitch (48 sts). To finish, sl st to first stitch of round.

Fasten off. Weave in ends.

Nose

Join Color C in any stitch on the last row.

Row 1: Ch1, sc 18 (18 sts).

Row 2: Turn, ch1, sc18 (18 sts).

Row 3: Turn, ch1, sc 18 (18 sts).

Row 4: Turn, sc dec, sc14, sc dec (16 sts).

Row 5: Turn, sc dec, sc12, sc dec (14 sts).

Row 6: Turn, sc dec, sc 10; sc dec (12 sts).

Fasten off, leaving a long tail to sew the nose down to the hat.

Flip the panel up onto the hat, and with yarn needle, sew all around the nose to secure it in place.

Nose Holes (make 2)

Using Color B, ch2.

Round 1: Sc6 in first chain. Sl st to first stitch to join (6 sts).

Fasten off, leaving a long tail to sew onto nose.

Horns (make 2)

Using Color B, ch2.

Round 1: Sc4 in first chain (4 sts).

Round 2: Working continuously in the round, 2sc in each stitch (8 sts).

Round 3: *Sc, 2sc in next stitch, repeat from * to complete round (12 sts).

Rounds 4–5: Sc12 (12 sts).

Round 6: *Sc, sc dec, repeat from * to complete round (9 sts).

Fasten off Color B; join Color A.

Rounds 7–12: Sc 9 (9 sts). To finish, sl st to first stitch of round.

Fasten off, leaving a long tail to sew horns onto hat.

Ears (make 2)

Using Color A, ch4.

Round 1: 4dc in first chain from hook, sl st to third chain to join round (5 sts).

Round 2: Ch3 (counts as first dc here and throughout), dc in same stitch, 2dc in next stitch and to complete round, sl st to third chain of ch3 to join (10 sts).

Round 3: Ch3, 2dc in next stitch, *dc, 2dc in next stitch, repeat from * to complete round, sl st to third chain of ch3 to join (15 sts).

Round 4: Ch3, dc in each stitch and to complete round, sl st to third chain of first ch3 to join (15 sts).

Round 5: Ch3, dc dec, *dc, dc dec, repeat from * to complete round, sl st to third chain of first ch3 to join (10 sts).

Round 6: Ch3, dc dec, *dc, dc dec, repeat from * to next to last stitch, dc in last stitch, sl st to third chain of first ch3 to join round (7 sts).

Fasten off, leaving a long tail to sew ear onto hat.

Finishing

Using yarn needle, sew the horns onto hat 1 row down from the top center. Sew the ears next to the horns and the nose holes onto the nose. Next, using the sewing needle and thread, securely sew the buttons on for the eyes. Weave in all ends.

What a Hoot! Owl Hat

Who has the cutest baby? You will, when your baby is wearing this super sweet owl hat!

Finished Measurements

Newborn: Circumference, 12–14"; Hat height, 5"
3–6 months: Circumference, 14–17"; Hat height, 5.5"
9–12 months: Circumference, 16–19"; Hat height, 6"

Yarn

- Red Heart Light & Lofty, super bulky weight #6 yarn, 100% acrylic (105 yd/4.5 oz per skein)
    - 1 skein #9965 Zebra Stripe (Color A)
- Lion Brand Vanna's Choice Baby, medium worsted weight #4 yarn, 100% acrylic (170 yd/3.5 oz per skein)
    - 1 skein #840-098 Lamb (Color B)
    - 1 skein #840-157 Duckie (Color C)
    - 1 skein #840-132 Goldfish (Color D)

Hook and Other Materials

- N-13 9mm hook or size needed to obtain gauge
- H-8 5mm hook or size needed to obtain gauge
- Stitch marker (optional)
- Yarn needle
- 2 small black buttons
- Sewing thread and needle

Gauge

Using Color A and N-13 9mm hook, 7 sts and 7 rows in sc = 3" square
Using Color B, C, or D and H-8 5mm hook, 11 sts and 13 rows in sc = 3" square

Notes

1. The hat is worked from the bottom up continuously in the round. If you like, mark the first stitch of the round with a stitch marker for reference.
2. The eyes, ears, and fringe are made separately and added last.

Special Technique

Fringe
It's so simple to add fringe to a hat or other garment for a bit of fun. You can follow these directions using any number of yarn strands cut to the same length and then folded in half together.

1. Insert the hook through the stitch where you wish the fringe to hang from the back of the stitch to the front, grab the center fold of the folded yarn strands, and pull through the stitch.

2. Pull the ends of the strands through the loops and pull tight.

Hat

Newborn

Using Color A and N-13 9mm hook, ch30, sl st to first chain to create a ring (30 sts).

Round 1: Ch1, sc in each stitch to complete round (30 sts).

Round 2: Working continuously in the round, sc in each stitch (30 sts).

Rounds 3–9: Sc in each stitch (30 sts).

Round 10: 2dc in each stitch (60 sts).

Rounds 11–12: Sc in each stitch (60 sts).

Fasten off, leaving a long tail to sew top of hat together.

3–6 Months

Using Color A and N-13 9mm hook, ch40, sl st to first chain to create a ring (40 sts).

Round 1: Ch1, sc in each stitch to complete round (40 sts).

Round 2: Working continuously in the round, sc in each stitch (40 sts).

Rounds 3–12: Sc in each stitch (40 sts).

Round 13: 2dc in each stitch (80 sts).

Rounds 14–15: Sc in each stitch (80 sts).

Fasten off, leaving a long tail to sew top of hat together.

9–12 Months

Using Color A and N-13 9mm hook, ch50, sl st to first chain to create a ring (50 sts).

Round 1: Ch1, sc in each stitch (50 sts).

Round 2: Working continuously in the round, sc in each stitch (50 sts).

Rounds 3–15: Sc in each stitch (50 sts)

Round 16: 2dc in each stitch (100 sts).

Rounds 17–18: Sc in each stitch (100 sts).

Fasten off, leaving a long tail to sew top of hat together.

For All Sizes

Fold the hat in half and use the yarn needle to sew the top of the hat together. The ears will naturally pull to each side.

Fasten off. Weave in ends.

Eyes (make 2 of each)

Back

Using Color B and H-8 5mm hook, ch2.

Round 1: 6sc in first chain (6 sts).

Round 2: Working continuously in the round, 2sc in each stitch (12 sts).

Round 3: *Sc, 2sc in next stitch, repeat from * to complete round (18 sts).

Round 4: *Sc2, 2sc in next stitch, repeat from * to complete round (24 sts).

Round 5: *Sc3, 2sc in next stitch, repeat from * to com-

plete round (32 sts). Sl st to first stitch of round. Fasten off. Weave in ends.

Top

Using Color C and H-8 5mm hook, ch2.

Round 1: 6sc in first chain (6 sts).

Round 2: Working continuously in the round, 2sc in each stitch (12 sts).

Round 3: *Sc, 2sc in next stitch, repeat from * to complete round (18 sts). Sl st to first stitch of round.

Fasten off. Weave in ends.

Beak

Using Color D and H-8 5mm hook, ch6.

Row 1: Turn, sc in first chain from hook and across (5 sts).

Row 2: Turn, sc in each stitch (5 sts).

Row 3: Turn, sc, sc dec, use middle stitch again and sc dec, sc (4 sts).

Row 4: Turn, sc dec, sc dec (2 sts).

Row 5: Turn, sc dec, ch1 (1 st).

Fasten off, leaving a long tail to sew onto hat.

Finishing

Using yarn needle, sew the back eyes onto the hat, followed by the top eyes. With the sewing needle, sew the buttons onto the top eyes as preferred (looking up, down, sideways, cross-eyed, etc.). Using the yarn needle, sew the beak in the center below the eyes. Fasten off. Weave in all ends.

Fringe on Ears

Cut three 4" lengths each of Colors B and C and add as you would like to each ear. Trim to same length.

Cotton Candy Hat

Cotton candy is sweet to eat, but it's even sweeter when worn!
This hat will perk up any outfit.

Finished Measurements
Newborn: Circumference, 12–14";
    Hat height, 5.5–6"
3–6 months: Circumference, 14–17";
    Hat height, 6.5–7"
9–12 months: Circumference, 16–19";
    Hat height, 7.5"

Yarn
- Yarn Bee Melody, bulky weight
  #5 yarn, 70% wool/30% acrylic
  (129 yd/4 oz per skein)
    1 skein #102 Floral (Color A)
- Red Heart Super Saver, medium
  worsted weight #4 yarn, 100%
  acrylic (364 yd/7 oz per skein)
    1 skein #718 Shocking Pink
      (Color B)
    1 skein #512 Turqua (Color C)

Hook and Other Materials
- H-8 5mm hook or size needed to
  obtain gauge
- Stitch marker (optional)
- Medium button
- Sewing thread and needle

Gauge
Using Color A, 6 sts and 8 rows in sc = 2" square

Notes
1. The hat is worked from the top down continuously in
   the round. If you like, mark the first stitch of the round
   with a stitch marker for reference.
2. The flowers will slip over the button and are removable.

Hat
Newborn
Using Color A, ch4, sl st to first chain to create a ring.
Round 1: Ch1 (this counts as your first sc), 7sc in ring
    (8 sts).
Round 2: Working continuously in the round, 2sc in each
    stitch (16 sts).
Round 3: *Sc, 2sc in next stitch, repeat from * to complete
    round (24 sts).
Round 4: *Sc2, 2sc in next stitch, repeat from * to com-
    plete round (32 sts).

Rounds 5–16: Sc in each stitch (32 sts). To finish, sl st to
    first stitch of round.
Fasten off. Weave in ends.

3–6 Months
Using Color A, ch4, sl st to first chain to create a ring.
Round 1: Ch1 (this counts as your first sc), 7sc in ring
    (8 sts).
Round 2: Working continuously in the round, 2sc in each
    stitch (16 sts).
Round 3: *Sc, 2sc in next stitch, repeat from * to complete
    round (24 sts).
Round 4: *Sc2, 2sc in next stitch, repeat from * to com-
    plete round (32 sts).
Round 5: *Sc3, 2sc in next stitch, repeat from * to com-
    plete round (40 sts).
Rounds 6–20: Sc in each stitch (40 sts). To finish, sl st to
    first stitch of round.
Fasten off. Weave in ends.

9–12 Months

Using Color A, ch4, sl st to first chain to create a ring.

Round 1: Ch1 (this counts as your first sc), 7sc in ring (8 sts).

Round 2: Working continuously in the round, 2sc in each stitch (16 sts).

Round 3: *Sc, 2sc in next stitch, repeat from * to complete round (24 sts).

Round 4: *Sc2, 2sc in next stitch, repeat from * to complete round (32 sts).

Round 5: *Sc3, 2sc in next stitch, repeat from * to complete round (40 sts).

Round 6: *Sc4, 2sc in next stitch, repeat from * to complete round (48 sts).

Rounds 7–24: Sc in each stitch (48 sts). To finish, sl st to first stitch of round.

Fasten off. Weave in ends.

Back Flower

Using Color C, ch4, sl st to first chain to create a ring.

Round 1: 9sc in ring, sl st to first stitch to join round (9 sts).

Round 2: *Ch10, sl st in same stitch, ch10, sl st in same stitch, sl st in next stitch, repeat from * to complete round.

Fasten off. Weave in ends.

Top Flower

Using Color B, ch4, sl st to first chain to create a ring.

Round 1: 9sc in ring, sl st to first stitch to join round (9 sts).

Round 2: *Ch6, sl st in same stitch, ch6, sl st in same stitch, sl st in next stitch, repeat from * to complete round.

Fasten off. Weave in ends.

Finishing

With sewing needle and thread, sew the button onto hat. Slip centers of flowers over button.